W9-DAN-961

A Guide to

AMERICAN STATES

New York

THE EMPIRE STATE

AV² provides enriched content that supplements and complements this book. Weigl's AV² books strive to create inspired learning and engage young minds in a total learning experience.

Your AV² Media Enhanced books come alive with...

Audio
Listen to sections of the book read aloud.

Key Words
Study vocabulary, and complete a matching word activity.

Video
Watch informative video clips.

Quizzes
Test your knowledge.

Embedded Weblinks
Gain additional information for research.

Slide Show
View images and captions, and prepare a presentation.

Try This!
Complete activities and hands-on experiments.

... and much, much more!

Go to **www.av2books.com**, and enter this book's unique code.

BOOK CODE

C 8 1 3 1 7 3

AV² by Weigl brings you media enhanced books that support active learning.

Published by AV² by Weigl
350 5th Avenue, 59th Floor
New York, NY 10118
Website: www.av2books.com   www.weigl.com

Library of Congress Cataloging-in-Publication Data

Lawton, Val.
 New York / Val Lawton.
    p. cm. -- (A guide to American states)
 Includes index.
 ISBN 978-1-61690-804-1 (hardcover : alk. paper) -- ISBN 978-1-61690-480-7 (online)
 1. New York (State)--Juvenile literature. I. Title.
 F119.3.L39 2011
 974.7--dc23
                              2011019033

Printed in the United States of America in North Mankato, Minnesota

052011
WEP180511

Project Coordinator Jordan McGill
Art Director Terry Paulhus

Photo Credits
Every reasonable effort has been made to trace ownership and to obtain permission to reprint copyright material. The publishers would be pleased to have any errors or omissions brought to their attention so that they may be corrected in subsequent printings.

Weigl acknowledges Getty Images as its primary image supplier for this title.

Contents

Nearly 3 miles of sandy beaches, amusement-park rides, and sports facilities make Coney Island a prime summer attraction.

Introduction

Few places in the United States can rival New York State's population, economic power, and cultural importance. The value of goods and services produced in the state is higher than that of most countries. From its sandy beaches and rugged mountains to the hustle and bustle of New York City, the state of New York is a place of sharp contrasts.

New York was one of the original 13 colonies. Its nickname, the Empire State, is thought to have come from George Washington, who called New York the "seat of empire." The people of New York have worked hard to live up to their state's nickname. Today, New York is a national leader in manufacturing, finance, education, and the arts.

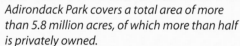
Adirondack Park covers a total area of more than 5.8 million acres, of which more than half is privately owned.

Rising on the site where the twin towers stood, the 1,776-foot-high One World Trade Center will be the tallest skyscraper in the United States.

New York has a rich and exciting history. It was first occupied by American Indians more than 10,000 years ago. The region was explored by the Italians and French, colonized by the Dutch, and then taken over by the English, who called their colony New York in honor of the duke of York. On July 26, 1788, New York entered the Union as the 11th state.

New York suffered a devastating blow on September 11, 2001, when terrorists flew two jet aircraft into the 110-story twin towers of the World Trade Center. The towers burned and collapsed, killing some 2,800 people in New York City. Many rescue workers showed great courage, putting their own lives at risk to save others. Recovering from the attack, the people of the city and state showed tremendous **resilience** and strength.

Where Is New York?

New York is part of the Middle Atlantic region of the United States. From southwest to northeast, New York is bordered by Lake Erie, the Canadian province of Ontario, Lake Ontario, and the Canadian province of Quebec. To the east are the New England states of Vermont, Massachusetts, and Connecticut. The Atlantic Ocean and New Jersey are to the southeast, and Pennsylvania is to the south.

There are many ways to get to the Empire State. The three largest airports that serve New York City are John F. Kennedy International Airport, LaGuardia Airport, and Newark Liberty International Airport, which is actually in neighboring New Jersey.

Buffalo's historic waterfront along Lake Erie is being redeveloped for recreation and tourism as well as commerce.

The New York City subway system extends 660 miles, includes 468 stations, and serves more than 1.5 billion riders each year.

The state is also reachable by car via many major highways, including the New York State Thruway, which links the New York City region with Albany, Syracuse, and Buffalo. New York has more than 110,000 miles of roads and highways. Trains serve many parts of the state and play an important role in transporting commuters to and from New York City and surrounding areas.

A key event in the history of the Empire State was the completion of the Erie Canal in 1825. It connected New York City with the Great Lakes via the Hudson River. The canal produced great revenues for the state and sped development of the American frontier. In 1918, the New York State Barge Canal was opened to replace the Erie Canal. This system, now known as the New York State Canal System, incorporates parts of the Erie Canal and supports much water traffic.

Mapping New York

The state of New York covers a total area of 54,556 square miles, making it the 27th largest state in the country. Land accounts for 47,214 square miles of New York's territory, with water making up the remaining 7,342 square miles. Parts of two of the Great Lakes, Ontario and Erie, account for more than half of the water area.

Sites and Symbols

STATE SEAL
New York

STATE BIRD
Eastern Bluebird

STATE FLOWER
Rose

STATE FLAG
New York

STATE ANIMAL
Beaver

STATE TREE
Sugar Maple

Nickname The Empire State

Motto *Excelsior* (Ever Upward)

Song "I Love New York," words and music by Steve Karmen

Entered the Union July 26, 1788, as the 11th state

Capital Albany

Population (2010 Census) 19,378,102 Ranked 3rd state

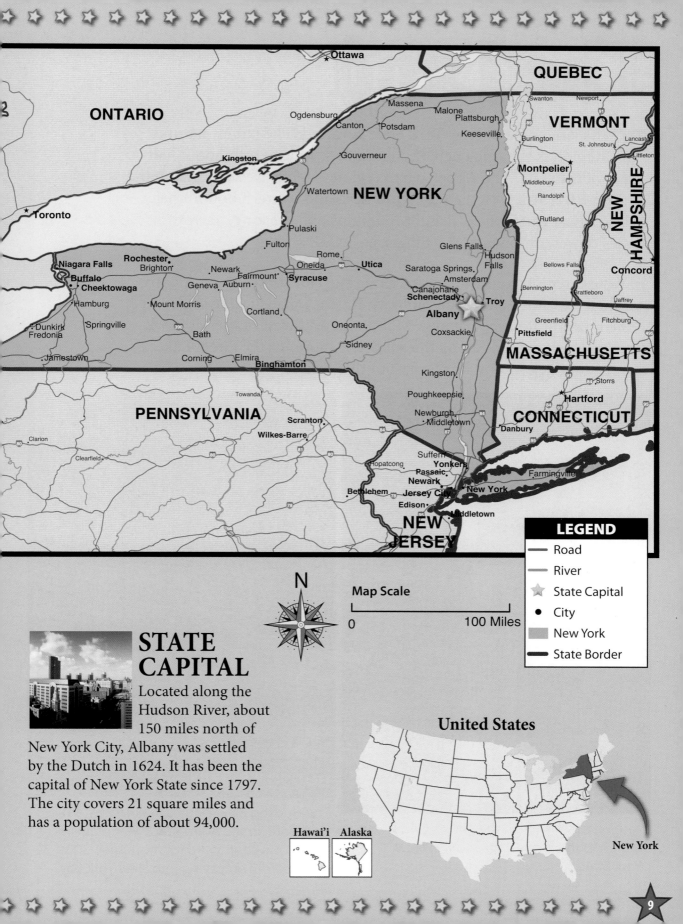

STATE CAPITAL

Located along the Hudson River, about 150 miles north of New York City, Albany was settled by the Dutch in 1624. It has been the capital of New York State since 1797. The city covers 21 square miles and has a population of about 94,000.

LEGEND

— Road
— River
⭐ State Capital
• City
▮ New York
— State Border

Map Scale

N

0   100 Miles

United States

Hawai'i   Alaska

New York

The Land

The landscape of New York State is varied. The largest natural region is the Appalachian Mountains, which cover about half of the state. The Appalachian region extends westward from the Hudson River valley to the state's southern and western boundaries. Within this area are the Catskill Mountains and the long, narrow bodies of water known as the Finger Lakes.

A lowland region runs northward along the Hudson River to Albany and then westward along the Mohawk River. A plateau-like region lies to the north of the Appalachian Mountains and west of the Mohawk River valley. It extends along the southern shores of the Great Lakes. The Adirondack Mountains lie east of this region.

TAUGHANNOCK FALLS

Taughannock Falls, in the Finger Lakes region, is the highest waterfall in New York State.

HUDSON RIVER

The Hudson River begins in northeastern New York, in the Adirondack Mountains. It then flows southward for more than 300 miles before emptying into New York Bay.

FINGER LAKES

Canadice Lake, one of the eleven Finger Lakes, is a primary source of drinking water for the city of Rochester.

MOUNT MARCY

The state's tallest peak, Mount Marcy, stands 5,344 feet high and is located in the Adirondacks.

The *Clearwater*, a Hudson River sailing vessel, promotes environmental education and helps raise funds to preserve and protect the river.

Long Island is 118 miles long and about 12 to 20 miles wide.

The principal rivers in New York State include the Mohawk, Hudson, Oswego, Genesee, Seneca, Delaware, and Allegheny.

Thousands of years ago, glaciers covered what is now New York, and their movement helped shape the land. Advancing and retreating glaciers carved out the state's many lakes.

Taughannock Falls is part of Taughannock State Park, about 8 miles north of Ithaca. The waterfall's 215-foot drop is 25 feet higher than the New York side of Niagara Falls.

Each winter, Buffalo usually receives close to 100 inches of snow.

Climate

N ew York State generally has warm summers and cold winters. Because of differences in altitude and location, the climate varies from region to region. The coldest part of the state is in the Champlain Valley. Here the average temperatures are about 10 degrees Fahrenheit lower than those in the New York City area. In midtown Manhattan, temperatures average 32.1° F in January and 76.5° F in July.

All parts of the state receive plenty of rain and snow. The area around Buffalo receives an unusually heavy amount of snowfall. Much of Buffalo's frozen precipitation is "lake effect" snow, which occurs when cold winds blow over the warmer waters of Lake Erie.

Average Annual Precipitation Across New York

As measured in Central Park, New York City receives 46 percent more precipitation each year than the Niagara Falls area. What factors might account for the difference?

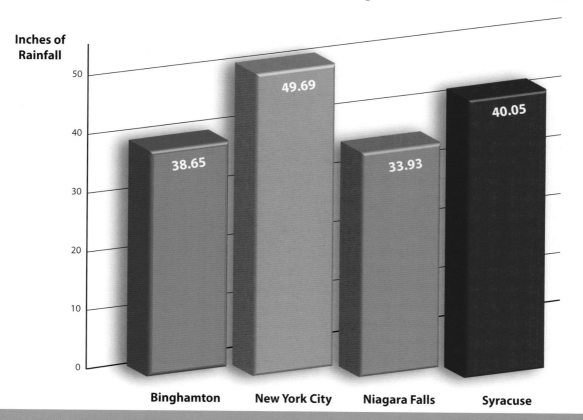

Inches of Rainfall

Binghamton	New York City	Niagara Falls	Syracuse
38.65	49.69	33.93	40.05

Natural Resources

One of New York's most important natural resources is water. The state has more than 8,000 lakes and many significant rivers. Some of New York's rivers provide **hydroelectric power** for homes and industry. In fact, the dam at Niagara Falls, located on the New York–Canadian border, is one of the largest producers of hydroelectricity in the world. The state also has a growing number of projects that use wind to produce electric power.

Water from the Niagara River and Falls supplies New York State with enough electricity to power 24 million 100-watt light bulbs simultaneously.

The state's inland and offshore waters support a commercial fishing industry. Major catches include clams, lobsters, squid, whiting, and flounder.

The mining industry supplies crushed stone, cement, sand, and gravel, all of which are used in construction. The state also produces significant amounts of salt and zinc. The country's only major wollastonite mine is located in New York. Wollastonite is used in ceramics, paints, and plastics.

At Lowville, agricultural land is also the site of a wind farm that can supply the annual electrical needs of more than 64,000 homes.

Anorthosite is a durable rock that can be used as a building material. New York's Mount Marcy and Whiteface Mountain are composed mainly of anorthosite.

New York's forests supply raw materials for the state's pulp and paper industry as well as hardwoods used to make furniture.

About 600,000 gallons of water fall over the cliffs of Niagara Falls each second.

The state gem is garnet, which is a red gemstone that is used in jewelry. When crushed, garnet is used as sandpaper.

Plants

New York State was once almost entirely forested. As people settled the area, they cleared some of the forestland for farms or to build cities and towns. Today, forests cover more than half of New York's land area, and they feature a rich mixture of **deciduous** and **coniferous** species. Some 150 kinds of trees grow in the state. Among the softwoods found in New York's forests are white pines, spruces, and hemlocks. Hardwood trees include beeches, oaks, and yellow birches.

New York's official state tree is the sugar maple, which grows in many parts of the state. The sugar maple produces sap that is tapped, collected, and boiled to make delicious maple syrup.

Many wild plants and flowers also grow throughout New York. Nearly 2,000 species of plants are native to the state. Flowering plants found in New York's forests include violets, bellworts, and hepaticas. In the spring, wildflowers such as buttercups, daisies, and asters decorate the state's meadows and hillsides.

SUGAR MAPLES

Sugar maples thrive in cool, moist climates and grow to heights of 40 to 80 feet.

LILAC

Known for its lovely, long-lasting fragrance, the lilac is the official state bush.

BELLWORTS

The large-flowered bellwort is a woodland wildflower that blooms between mid-April and mid-May.

PINK LADY'S SLIPPER

A member of the orchid family, the pink lady's slipper is found in a wide variety of New York habitats.

I DIDN'T KNOW THAT!

About 60 species of wild orchids grow in New York.

The first commercial apple tree nursery in colonial America was established in New York in 1730.

Rochester hosts an annual lilac festival. The flowers displayed at the city's Highland Park include more than 500 lilac varieties on more than 1,200 bushes.

The rose became the official state flower in 1955.

Thanks to a law passed in the 1890s, much of Adirondack Park, the state's largest forest preserve, will remain wild forever.

Animals

New York is home to a large variety of wildlife. Small mammals such as the deer mouse, eastern cottontail, snowshoe hare, woodchuck, gray squirrel, muskrat, and raccoon are common. Larger mammals include the white-tailed deer, beaver, and black bear. Many mammals such as the cougar and gray wolf have been subject to overhunting and no longer are found in the wild in the state. Various wildlife management programs work to protect or reestablish certain animal populations. The state is home to many types of birds. The common house sparrow was introduced to the New York City area from Europe in the early 1850s.

New York's waters host an abundance of aquatic life. Many different species of freshwater fish are found in the state's lakes and rivers. These fish include bass, perch, pickerel, and trout. In the ocean, tuna, bass, flounder, and different kinds of shellfish may be found. The state's coastal waters also provide habitat for whales, dolphins, and seals.

SNOWSHOE HARE

Brown in summer, the snowshoe hare's coat turns white in winter, providing camouflage from predators.

RACCOON

Raccoons thrive in a wide variety of habitats throughout New York State.

HOUSE SPARROW

Abundant in New York, the common house sparrow usually makes its home in cities, suburbs, and towns, as well as other human settlements.

DOLPHIN

Dolphins, found in the Atlantic Ocean and Long Island Sound, are protected by federal law.

Tourism

The state of New York is one of the most popular tourist destinations in the United States. Each year, more than 45 million tourists visit New York City to see the bright lights of Manhattan. Of these visitors, nearly 37 million come from the United States and more than 8 million come from other countries. Tourists also enjoy the vast wilderness of the Adirondacks, the beaches of Long Island, and Chautauqua County's excellent birdwatching opportunities.

One of the state's greatest tourist draws is the world-renowned Niagara Falls. These impressive falls are popular among newlyweds as a honeymoon destination. On the New York side, the falls are called the American Falls, and they cascade from a height of about 180 feet. Visitors can travel beneath the falls aboard the *Maid of the Mist*, a steamboat service that has been in operation since 1846. Sightseers on the *Maid of the Mist* get close enough to the falls to need rain gear to keep their clothes dry.

TIMES SQUARE

Dozens of theaters, restaurants, and other attractions cluster around Times Square, in the heart of New York City.

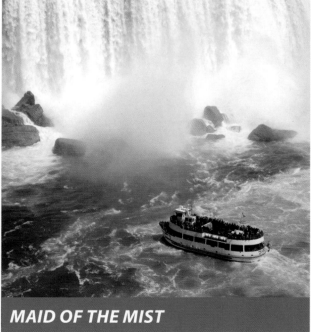

MAID OF THE MIST

Since the mid-1800s, eleven Niagara Falls tour boats have carried the name *Maid of the Mist*. Four are still in service.

CENTRAL PARK

Attracting about 25 million people annually, New York City's Central Park is the nation's most visited urban park.

UNITED NATONS

The United Nations has its headquarters on an 18-acre site in Manhattan, next to the East River.

New York City's Central Park is a popular site for both tourists and locals. Built beginning in the 1850s, the park covers 840 acres and extends north-south for more than 50 blocks.

Tarrytown, just north of New York City, was settled by the Dutch in the 1600s. The area is now a popular tourist site that includes Sleepy Hollow, where the fictional Ichabod Crane was chased by the Headless Horseman in "The Legend of Sleepy Hollow," a tale written by Washington Irving.

The Old Dutch Reformed Church in Tarrytown was built in the 1680s. Now restored, it is a national historic landmark.

Although located in New York City, the United Nations is considered to be international territory. The UN site has its own post office branch and its own firefighting force.

Industry

Now York is a major manufacturing center with more than 18,000 factories. These factories produce such items as electrical and medical equipment, computer equipment, clothing, plastics, chemicals, and **pharmaceuticals**. Many leading U.S. companies have their headquarters in New York City. The city is also a center of the media and entertainment industry. Many films and television programs are made in New York City's studios or use the city as a background.

Industries in New York
Value of Goods and Services in Millions of Dollars

Besides manufacturing, the finance, media, and tourism industries are very important to the state's economy. What categories in the pie chart reflect the importance of tourism?

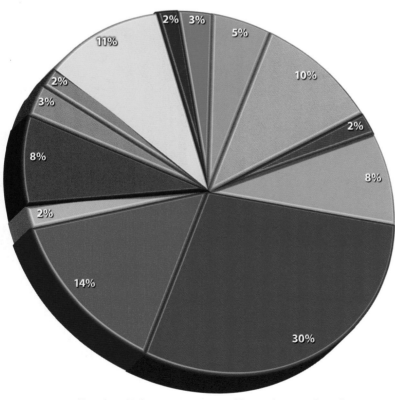

LEGEND

* Agriculture, Forestry, and Fishing	$1,986
* Mining	$990
■ Utilities	$19,058
■ Construction	$36,719
■ Manufacturing	$58,485
■ Wholesale and Retail Trade	$107,654
■ Transportation	$19,231
■ Media and Entertainment	$90,794
■ Finance, Insurance, and Real Estate	$327,930
■ Professional and Technical Services	$150,388
■ Education	$19,324
■ Health Care	$83,577
■ Hotels and Restaurants	$28,709
■ Other Services	$25,435
■ Government	$122,939
TOTAL	**$1,093,219**

*Less than 1%. Percentages may not add to 100 because of rounding.

More than 870,000 people buy the New York Times *newspaper each day. Millions more read the* Times *online.*

Agriculture is important to New York's economy. Dairy farming is particularly significant. The state ranks second to Vermont in maple syrup production. Floriculture, the growing of decorative plants, also contributes to the economy.

Goods and Services

New York provides the nation with a variety of goods, from fresh fruit to fashionable clothing to state-of-the-art electronic equipment. Many of New York's goods are exported to other states and countries. The state's excellent transportation system makes it a leader in distribution. Busy port facilities in places such as the New York City **metropolitan area**, Buffalo, and Albany handle many of these goods.

New York is the center of commerce and finance in the United States. The city's financial district, which is centered on Manhattan's Wall Street, is home to some of the world's most powerful banks, brokerage firms, and stock exchanges. The New York Stock Exchange is a driving force in the nation's economy. The exchange evolved from a meeting in 1792, when 24 New York City stockbrokers and merchants came together for trading purposes. Formally opened in 1817 as the New York Stock and Exchange Board, it remains one of the world's largest and most influential securities markets. NASDAQ, also headquartered in New York City, is another stock exchange with worldwide influence.

The New York Stock Exchange trades shares of more than 2,300 companies with a combined market value of more than $13 trillion.

About 1,000 cadets graduate each year from the U.S. Military Academy at West Point.

The State University of New York, created in 1948, is one of the world's largest educational organizations. Its many state-supported institutions of higher learning include major university centers at Stony Brook, Albany, Binghamton, and Buffalo. Many colleges that receive both state and local funds belong to a system known as the City University of New York.

New York's best-known private schools for higher education include Columbia University and the Juilliard School of Music, both in New York City, and Cornell University, in Ithaca. The federal government operates the U.S. Military Academy at West Point and the U.S. Merchant Marine Academy at Kings Point on Long Island.

American Indians

People have lived in the New York region for more than 10,000 years. American Indians were the first to inhabit the area. **Archaeological** evidence suggests that more than 8,000 early American Indians lived along the banks of the lower Hudson River and on Staten, Long, and Manhattan islands.

By the late 1500s, two major Indian groups, the Algonquian-speaking peoples and the Iroquois Confederacy, inhabited much of New York. The Algonquian peoples included the Mahican, or Mohican, and the Munsee. These groups lived chiefly in the Hudson Valley and on Long Island. Algonquian groups built and lived in long wooden structures called longhouses. These structures were often home to more than 50 people.

In the Hudson River valley, the Indians sold furs to the Dutch in exchange for beads, brandy, knives, and other items.

The Iroquois were very powerful, and they often fought with the neighboring Algonquian peoples.

The Iroquois Confederacy was known as the Five Nations from 1570 until 1722, when the Tuscarora joined. The Confederacy then became known as the Six Nations.

The name "Manhattan" is an Algonquian word meaning "hilly island."

The Iroquois Confederacy, formed in 1570, originally included the Mohawk, the Oneida, the Onondaga, the Cayuga, and the Seneca. Like the Algonquian peoples, the Iroquois established farming communities and lived in longhouses. Each Iroquois community had a ruling council and a village chief, while the entire Iroquois Confederacy was run by a council of delegates.

More than 1,000 American Indian artists, performers, and educators gather at Floyd Bennett Field in Brooklyn for the annual Gateway to Nations festival.

Located on the border between New York and Vermont, Lake Champlain is named for the Frenchman who was the first European to explore and map it.

Explorers

The first European to visit the New York area was probably an Italian navigator, Giovanni da Verrazzano. Hired by the king of France to explore North America, Verrazzano sailed into New York harbor in 1524. He left, however, without exploring the region.

In 1609, the French explorer Samuel de Champlain reached the lake that was later named after him. That same year, Henry Hudson, an English explorer, sailed up what was later named the Hudson River and claimed the land for the Netherlands. Employed by the Dutch East India Company, Hudson was assigned to find the Northwest Passage. This was a water route that was thought to exist and that would provide a shortcut to Asia. Although he did not find such a route, he wrote a report describing the New York area. This report generated interest from his employers in the Netherlands, and soon the Dutch claimed much of the New York region. The Dutch named the area New Netherland and began building permanent settlements.

Timeline of Settlement

Early Exploration

1524 Giovanni da Verrazzano enters New York harbor.

1609 Samuel de Champlain explores the area of northeastern New York, and Henry Hudson explores the Hudson River region.

First Colonies Established

1614 The Dutch build Fort Nassau near the site of present-day Albany. It is washed out by a flood.

1626 Peter Minuit, the Dutch colonial governor, purchases Manhattan from the Lenape Indians.

1664 The English take control of the Dutch colony of New Netherland and rename it New York.

1625 The Dutch settlement of New Amsterdam is founded at the southern end of Manhattan island.

American Revolution

1776 As one of the original 13 colonies, New York signs the Declaration of Independence and joins the fight for freedom from British rule.

1776 British forces drive General George Washington's army out of the New York City area. The British occupy the city for the rest of the war.

1777 American forces defeat the British in the Battle of Saratoga, an important victory that helped the Americans win their independence several years later.

Statehood and Civil War

1788 New York ratifies the Constitution and joins the Union as a state.

1789 President George Washington is inaugurated in New York City, the first capital of the United States.

1825 The Erie Canal is completed.

1861–1865 Although the state sides with the Union during the Civil War, some New Yorkers riot against the military draft.

Early Settlers

N ew Netherland's first permanent settlement was established by the Dutch West India Company in 1624. Most of the settlers were French Huguenots. These people were Protestants who had fled religious **persecution** in France. The Huguenots established Fort Orange in the northern Hudson Valley, at present-day Albany.

Map of Settlements and Resources in Early New York

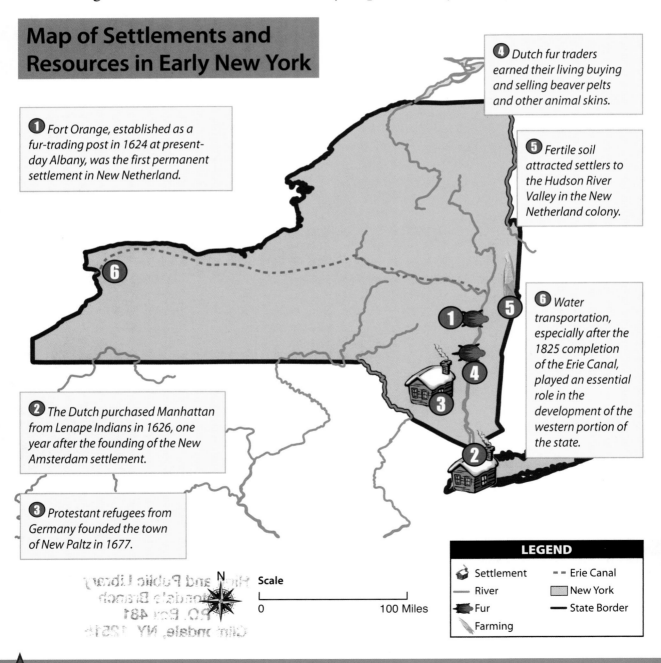

4 Dutch fur traders earned their living buying and selling beaver pelts and other animal skins.

1 Fort Orange, established as a fur-trading post in 1624 at present-day Albany, was the first permanent settlement in New Netherland.

5 Fertile soil attracted settlers to the Hudson River Valley in the New Netherland colony.

6 Water transportation, especially after the 1825 completion of the Erie Canal, played an essential role in the development of the western portion of the state.

2 The Dutch purchased Manhattan from Lenape Indians in 1626, one year after the founding of the New Amsterdam settlement.

3 Protestant refugees from Germany founded the town of New Paltz in 1677.

Scale

0   100 Miles

N

LEGEND

Settlement	- - Erie Canal
— River	New York
Fur	— State Border
Farming	

In 1625, the Dutch expanded their New Netherland colony with the founding of New Amsterdam, on the southern tip of Manhattan Island. The New Netherland settlements grew slowly at first. To spur immigration, the Dutch West India Company offered large tracts of cheap land in 1629 to anyone who would bring 50 settlers to the colony within four years. Such people, known as patroons, became owners of vast amounts of land. They then rented plots of farmland to tenants. Unlike other colonies in North America, New Netherland tolerated all nationalities and religions. As a result, people from many different groups moved there.

The English took control of New Netherland in 1664. The colony was renamed New York in honor of the duke of York. In 1683, representatives of the colony drew up the Charter of Liberties and Privileges, the first bill of rights in America. The colony grew rapidly between 1700 and the beginning of the American Revolution in 1775, reaching a population of more than 160,000.

Dutch Governor Peter Stuyvesant surrendered New Amsterdam to the English on September 8, 1664.

Notable People

Two of the nation's most celebrated presidents were born in New York. The state has also been home to African American leaders, medical pioneers, and influential and extremely successful leaders in business and entertainment.

SOJOURNER TRUTH (c. 1797–1883)

Born into slavery at a time when it was legal in New York State, Sojourner Truth escaped to freedom in 1826. She spent much of her adult life traveling from town to town, campaigning against slavery and for women's rights. A gifted preacher and singer, she also worked in Washington, D.C. during and after the Civil War to help slaves freed from the South.

THEODORE ROOSEVELT (1858–1919)

A native of New York City, Theodore Roosevelt became a military hero during the Spanish-American War. He served as governor of New York and was elected U.S. vice president in 1898. He became president after William McKinley was shot to death in 1901. "TR" helped to preserve the nation's forests and wilderness areas, and he fought to limit the power of big corporations.

FRANKLIN D. ROOSEVELT (1882–1945)

Born in Hyde Park, Franklin Roosevelt was stricken with polio in 1921 but fought back to overcome his disability. Like his distant cousin Theodore Roosevelt, "FDR" became governor of New York and U.S. president. Elected to a record four terms, he guided the country through the Great Depression of the 1930s and World War II.

JONAS SALK (1914–1995)

Born to Russian-Jewish immigrants in New York City, Jonas Salk was the first member of his family to attend college and become a doctor. In the 1940s and 1950s, he developed a vaccine against polio, a disease that had killed or crippled many thousands of children. He spent the rest of his life working on ways to protect people against other diseases.

COLIN POWELL (1937–)

After growing up in New York City, Colin Powell joined the U.S. Army and fought in the Vietnam War. He was the first African American to serve as chairman of the joint chiefs of staff, the nation's highest-ranking military officer. After leaving the military, he became the nation's first African American secretary of state.

I DIDN'T KNOW THAT!

Michael Bloomberg (1942–) was first elected mayor of New York City in 2001 and won reelection twice. He is also one of the richest people in the world. As the founder of a financial news and information service, he is worth an estimated $18 billion and has given nearly $1 billion to charity.

Jay-Z (1969–) grew up in Brooklyn and began his career as a rapper. With U.S. sales of more than 27 million albums, Jay-Z has also become a successful recording executive and part-owner of the New Jersey Nets of the National Basketball Association.

Population

The population of New York is exceptionally diverse. Millions of people, representing every ethnic group, entered the country through immigration stations at Castle Garden and Ellis Island in the 1800s and early 1900s, and many chose to stay in the state. Even today, people born outside the United States make up about 20 percent of the state's population.

New York is home to more than 19.3 million people and is one of the most densely populated states in the country. Compared to the national average of about 87 people per square mile of land area, New York State has about 410 people per square mile.

New York Population 1950–2010

Although the population of New York State increased by more than 30 percent between 1950 and 2010, this growth has not been continuous. In what decade did New York actually lose population? What factors might account for this period of decline?

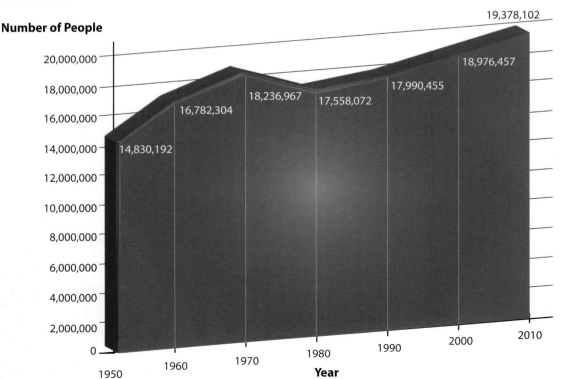

Number of People

- 14,830,192
- 16,782,304
- 18,236,967
- 17,558,072
- 17,990,455
- 18,976,457
- 19,378,102

Year: 1950, 1960, 1970, 1980, 1990, 2000, 2010

More than 100 million Americans can trace their ancestry to someone who came through Ellis Island's immigration processing center.

More than 40 percent of all state residents live in one of the five boroughs of New York City. The five boroughs are Manhattan, Brooklyn, the Bronx, Queens, and Staten Island. Most of the city's foremost financial, commercial, educational, and cultural institutions are in Manhattan. The other four boroughs, sometimes described as the outer boroughs, are mostly residential. Many people who live in the outer boroughs and surrounding suburbs travel to work in Manhattan by subway, bus, commuter train, or car. Other leading population centers in the state include Buffalo, Rochester, Yonkers, Syracuse, and Albany, the state capital.

New York's second-largest city is Buffalo, with about 270,000 residents.

Because of its historical importance, Ellis Island was made part of the Statue of Liberty National Monument in 1965.

About 10 percent of New York City dwellers are Jewish.

The New York City borough with the most people is Brooklyn, which has more than 2.5 million residents living within its 71 square miles. Many Brooklyn streets are lined with multistory brick or stone buildings known as brownstones.

Politics and Government

N ew York's first constitution was adopted in 1777. Under this constitution, George Clinton became the state's first governor to be directly elected by the people. New York's current constitution was adopted in 1894 and extensively revised in 1938. It has been amended many times.

Constructed between 1867 and 1899, the state capitol building in Albany cost about $25 million, a very large sum for that time.

Andrew Cuomo served as New York's attorney general before being sworn in as governor in January 2011.

The state government is divided into executive, legislative, and judicial branches. The governor heads the executive branch and serves a term of four years. The governor is responsible for proposing the state budget, appointing state department directors, and signing bills into law.

New York's legislative branch makes the laws. The state legislature has two parts, or chambers. There is a 62-member Senate and a 150-member Assembly. Senators and assembly members serve two-year terms. The judicial branch interprets and enforces the state's laws.

The Democratic Party has long been a powerful force in New York City politics. One of the most popular political leaders in recent New York State history was Mario Cuomo, a Democrat who served three four-year terms as governor, from 1983 through 1994. His son, Andrew Cuomo, was elected governor in November 2010.

I DIDN'T KNOW THAT!

New York's state song is called "I Love New York."

Here are the words to the entire song:

I LOVE NEW YORK
[repeat three times]
There isn't another like it
No matter where you go
And nobody can compare it
It's win and place and show
New York is special
New York is diff'rent
'Cause there's no place
else on earth
Quite like New York
And that's why
I LOVE NEW YORK
[repeat three times]

New York State is divided into 62 counties.

The Court of Appeals is New York's highest court. It consists of a chief judge and six associate judges who are appointed by the governor for 14-year terms.

Cultural Groups

N ew York is home to a broad range of cultural groups. Throughout the state's history, immigrants from many different countries have chosen to make their home in New York. The earliest European settlers came from the Netherlands, England, Scotland, and Germany. Throughout the 1700s, 1800s, and early 1900s, the largest groups of immigrants arriving in New York came from Russia, Poland, Ireland, Austria, Canada, and England. Italy, Germany, and Romania also provided large numbers of newcomers. Later in the 20th century and in the early 21st century, immigrants came in great numbers from Africa, Asia, Central and South America, and the Caribbean islands. Immigration has made New York City the most culturally diverse city in the United States.

New York City's annual St. Patrick's Day parade attracts more than 150,000 marchers and dancers, along with some 2 million spectators.

New York City's large West Indian community holds an annual carnival in Brooklyn.

Today, New York's largest minority groups are Hispanics and African Americans. In the Bronx, Latinos make up more than half the total population. People of Asian ancestry make up a growing share of the population of New York City.

New York State is home to more than 80,000 American Indians. Many are descendants of the Six Nations of the Iroquois Confederacy. The Seneca and Mohawk are the largest of these groups. Three Seneca **reservations** are located in western New York, and the Mohawk have land in the northern part of the state. The Oneida Nation is also part of the Iroquois Confederacy. Today, people of the Oneida Nation live in central New York.

Like the state's American Indians, many of New York's other cultural groups honor and celebrate their own traditions. For example, New York City hosts the world's largest St. Patrick's Day Parade. Many other groups, including Puerto Ricans, Chinese Americans, and Italian Americans, also hold colorful parades and festivals, both in New York City and throughout the state.

I DIDN'T KNOW THAT!

Writer Alex Haley, best known for *Roots*, a saga of African American life, was born in Ithaca.

Many African Americans seeking better working and social conditions came to New York in the early 1900s. Harlem, a Manhattan neighborhood, is a major center of African American culture in the United States.

The Puerto Rican Day Parade in New York City was first held in 1958. It attracts about 100,000 marchers and millions of spectators.

Each year, Syracuse hosts the Central New York Scottish Games and Celtic Festival. The event features bagpipe music, Scottish food, Highland and Irish dancing, and traditional athletic competitions.

Arts and Entertainment

New York is a leading center for the arts. In the 1800s, the Hudson River valley's scenery inspired artists such as Thomas Cole to paint beautiful landscapes of the valley and the Catskill Mountains. Their painting style later became known as the Hudson River School. In the 1940s, artists working, living, or exhibiting in New York City developed a style known as **abstract expressionism**, which dominated Western art during the next decade. In the 1960s, New York–based Andy Warhol and Robert Rauschenberg were leaders in the creation of **pop art**. The state's visual artists continue to be innovators in the art world.

Since the 1890s, Manhattan's Broadway has been among the world's leading theater districts. Stage performers from around the world often dream of performing on Broadway. New York City's Carnegie Hall, which opened in 1891, has hosted many of the world's greatest classical musicians.

Built in the 1960s, Lincoln Center for the Performing Arts is the home of the Metropolitan Opera, New York Philharmonic, and New York City Ballet.

Many celebrated writers and entertainers have links to the Empire State. Walt Whitman, considered by many to be the nation's greatest poet, was born on Long Island in 1819. Other important New York authors include Herman Melville, who wrote the great whaling adventure *Moby Dick*, and Washington Irving, a popular essayist and short-story writer. Edith Wharton, author of *The Age of Innocence*, was the first woman to receive a Pulitzer Prize. Playwrights from New York include Eugene O'Neill, Arthur Miller, and Neil Simon.

Actor and director Woody Allen, comedian Jerry Seinfeld, and singer Barbra Streisand are all entertainers from New York City. Other New York natives include comedian Rosie O'Donnell, singer Billy Joel, rock musician Lou Reed, and movie star Tom Cruise.

Jerry Seinfeld starred as himself in "Seinfeld," a long-running television comedy series set in New York City. His co-stars included another New Yorker, Julia Louis-Dreyfus, along with Jason Alexander and Michael Richards.

Sports

New Yorkers enjoy a variety of outdoor activities. In the warmer months, outdoor enthusiasts flock to the state's mountains and forests to go hiking, camping, or mountain climbing. Boating, fishing, and swimming are popular pastimes at Lake George, the Thousand Islands, and the Finger Lakes. The Hudson River offers canoeing and whitewater rafting, while sailing is a favorite activity off the Atlantic coast. In the winter, New York's snow-covered mountains provide great opportunities for skiing, snowboarding, and tobogganing, and its many wilderness trails are ideal for cross-country skiing and snowmobiling.

Each fall, up to 45,000 runners, including many of the world's best, compete in the New York City Marathon.

Lake Placid, which hosted the Winter Olympics in 1932 and 1980, continues to attract world-class skiers.

Professional sports are very popular in New York. The state has three professional National Hockey League teams, the Buffalo Sabres, the New York Rangers, and the New York Islanders. Pro football fans throughout the state cheer for three teams in the National Football League, the Buffalo Bills, the New York Giants, and the New York Jets. The New York Knicks play in the National Basketball Association, and the New York Liberty compete in the Women's National Basketball Association.

Known throughout the world, the New York Yankees have been the most successful team in Major League Baseball history. Some of baseball's greatest players, including Babe Ruth, Lou Gehrig, Joe DiMaggio, Mickey Mantle, and Alex Rodriguez, have worn the Yankee pinstripes. New York's other Major League Baseball team, the Mets, play their home games at Citi Field in Queens.

After joining the Yankees in 2004, Alex Rodriguez was twice named the American League's most valuable player.

National Averages Comparison

The United States is a federal republic, consisting of fifty states and the District of Columbia. Alaska and Hawai'i are the only non-contiguous, or non-touching, states in the nation. Today, the United States of America is the third-largest country in the world in population. The United States Census Bureau takes a census, or count of all the people, every ten years. It also regularly collects other kinds of data about the population and the economy. How does New York compare to the national average?

Comparison Chart

Statistic	USA	New York
Admission to Union	NA	July 26, 1788
Land Area (in square miles)	3,537,438.44	47,213.79
Population Total	308,745,538	19,378,102
Population Density (people per square mile)	87.28	410.43
Population Percentage Change (April 1, 2000, to April 1, 2010)	9.7%	2.1%
White Persons (percent)	72.4%	65.7%
Black Persons (percent)	12.6%	15.9%
American Indian and Alaska Native Persons (percent)	0.9%	0.6%
Asian Persons (percent)	4.8%	7.3%
Native Hawaiian and Other Pacific Islander Persons (percent)	0.2%	—
Some Other Race (percent)	6.2%	7.4%
Persons Reporting Two or More Races (percent)	2.9%	3.0%
Persons of Hispanic or Latino Origin (percent)	16.3%	17.6%
Not of Hispanic or Latino Origin (percent)	83.7%	82.4%
Median Household Income	$52,029	$55,980
Percentage of People Age 25 or Over Who Have Graduated from High School	80.4%	79.1%

*All figures are based on the 2010 United States Census, with the exception of the last two items. Percentages may not add to 100 because of rounding.

How to Improve My Community

Strong communities make strong states. Think about what features are important in your community. What do you value? Education? Health? Forests? Safety? Beautiful spaces? Government works to help citizens create ideal living conditions that are fair to all by providing services in communities. Consider what changes you could make in your community. How would they improve your state as a whole? Using this concept web as a guide, write a report that outlines the features you think are most important in your community and what improvements could be made. A strong state needs strong communities.

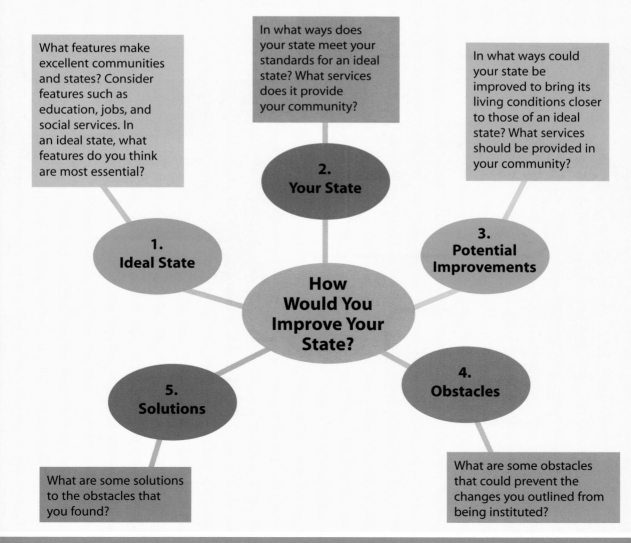

What features make excellent communities and states? Consider features such as education, jobs, and social services. In an ideal state, what features do you think are most essential?

In what ways does your state meet your standards for an ideal state? What services does it provide your community?

In what ways could your state be improved to bring its living conditions closer to those of an ideal state? What services should be provided in your community?

2. Your State

1. Ideal State

3. Potential Improvements

How Would You Improve Your State?

5. Solutions

4. Obstacles

What are some solutions to the obstacles that you found?

What are some obstacles that could prevent the changes you outlined from being instituted?

Exercise Your Mind!

Think about these questions and then use your research skills to find the answers and learn more fascinating facts about New York. A teacher, librarian, or parent may be able to help you locate the best sources to use in your research.

1 The Erie Canal ran between which two cities in New York?

2 Why is the name David Letterman associated with New York City?

3 True or False? The very first pizzeria in the United States was established in New York City.

4 True or False? The state flag of New York bears the image of justice with a hand over her mouth.

5 A farmer's field just outside of Bethel, in New York's Catskills, was the scene of which famous music festival in 1969?

a) The US Music Festival
b) Lilith Fair
c) The Woodstock Music and Arts Fair
d) The Monterey International Pop Festival

6 What famous academy is located at West Point?

7 Soho is a district in New York City. What does the word stand for?

8 Approximately what percentage of the state's residents live in New York City?

a. 20 percent
b. 40 percent
c. 60 percent
d. 80 percent

Words to Know

abstract expressionism: an artistic style developed in the 1940s that used bold and unusual brush strokes, including paint splattering and solid fields of color

archaeological: having to do with the study of ancient artifacts

coniferous: types of trees that bear cones and are usually evergreens

deciduous: types of trees that shed their leaves annually

hydroelectric power: electricity generated using the power of moving water

inauguration: formal induction into political office

metropolitan area: a large city and its surrounding communities

persecution: harassing or subjecting people to ill-treatment based on their religion, race, place of origin, or beliefs

pharmaceuticals: medicinal drugs

pop art: art movement born in New York City in the 1960s that used images borrowed from popular culture, such as soup cans, comic strips, and road signs

reservations: lands set aside for use by American Indians

resilience: the ability to rebound quickly from misfortune or defeat

Index

Log on to www.av2books.com

AV² by Weigl brings you media enhanced books that support active learning. Go to www.av2books.com, and enter the special code found on page 2 of this book. You will gain access to enriched and enhanced content that supplements and complements this book. Content includes video, audio, web links, quizzes, a slide show, and activities.

Audio
Listen to sections of the book read aloud.

Video
Watch informative video clips.

Embedded Weblinks
Gain additional information for research.

Try This!
Complete activities and hands-on experiments.

WHAT'S ONLINE?

 Try This!

Test your knowledge of the state in a mapping activity.

Find out more about precipitation in your city.

Plan what attractions you would like to visit in the state.

Learn more about the early natural resources of the state.

Write a biography about a notable resident of New York.

Complete an educational census activity.

 Embedded Weblinks

Discover more attractions in New York.

Learn more about the history of the state.

Learn the full lyrics of the state song.

Video

Watch a video introduction to New York.

Watch a video about the features of the state.

EXTRA FEATURES

Audio
Listen to sections of the book read aloud.

Key Words
Study vocabulary, and complete a matching word activity.

Slide Show
View images and caption and prepare a presentatic

Quizzes
Test your knowledge.

AV² was built to bridge the gap between print and digital. We encourage you to tell us what you like and what you want to see in the future.

Sign up to be an AV² Ambassador at www.av2books.com/ambassador.